P9-ECP-536

First Facts®

Christmas around the World

Christmas in
ENGLAND

by Cheryl L. Enderlein

CAPSTONE PRESS
a capstone imprint

First Facts are published by Capstone Press,
1710 Roe Crest Drive, North Mankato, Minnesota 56003
www.capstonepub.com

Library of Congress Cataloging-in-Publication Data
Enderlein, Cheryl L.
Christmas in England / by Cheryl L. Enderlein.
p. cm.— (First facts. Christmas around the world)
Includes bibliographical references and index.
Summary: "Describes the customs, songs, foods, and activities associated with the celebration of
Christmas in England"—Provided by publisher.
ISBN 978-1-62065-141-4 (library binding)
ISBN 978-1-4765-1060-6 (ebook PDF)
1. Christmas--England—Juvenile literature. 2. England—Social life and customs—Juvenile
literature. I. Title.

GT4987.44.E64 2013
394.26630942—dc23   2012026286

Editorial Credits
Christine Peterson, editor; Ted Williams, designer; Eric Gohl, media researcher; Kathy McColley,
production specialist

Photo Credits
Alamy: Beata Moore, 15, T.M.O.Pictures, 17; Capstone Studio: Karon Dubke, 21; Getty Images:
Gary John Norman, cover, Paul Harris, 12; iStockphotos: 5, AlbanyPictures, 11; Newscom: Robert
Harding/Adam Woolfitt, 8, 20; Shutterstock: Bikeworldtravel, 1, Christopher Elwell, 18, Ramon
Grosso Dolarea, 6

Design Elements: Shutterstock

Printed in the United States of America in North Mankato, Minnesota.
062016   009858R

TABLE OF CONTENTS

Christmas in England

Father Christmas fills stockings with gifts. Christmas crackers pop open with surprises. Families gather around Yule logs. These are a few of the sights and sounds of Christmas in England. On December 25, people in England celebrate with food, gifts, and other **traditions**.

tradition—a custom, idea, or belief passed down through time

England

How to Say It!
In England, people say "Happy Christmas" or "Merry Christmas."

CHRISTMAS FACT!

Today Bethlehem is located in an area of the Middle East called the West Bank.

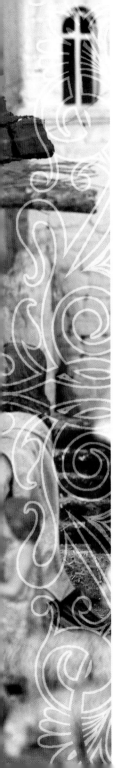

The First Christmas

Christians celebrate the birth of **Jesus** on Christmas. Long ago, Mary and her husband, Joseph, went to the town of Bethlehem. Mary was going to have a baby. When they got to Bethlehem, the couple had no place to stay. They spent the night in a stable where Jesus was born.

Christian—a person who follows a religion based on the teachings of Jesus
Jesus—the founder of the Christian religion

Christmas Celebrations

On Christmas Day English families go to church. Then they share a large midday meal. Children have to wait until after the meal to open their presents. People also listen to a holiday greeting given by Queen Elizabeth II.

The English celebrate Boxing Day on December 26. On this day people get the day off from work and school. They give money, food, or gifts to those who have helped them during the year. People watch soccer games, go shopping, and visit friends.

CHRISTMAS FACT!

Some say Boxing Day was named for an English tradition. On December 26, workers would get gift boxes from people they served that year.

Christmas Symbols

Crackle, crackle, pop! That's the sound of a Christmas cracker opening. Christmas crackers aren't food. These colorful tubes covered with paper remind English people of a crackling fire.

On Christmas Day everyone gets a cracker at dinnertime. Each person pulls the ends of the tube, and the cracker pops open. Inside the crackers are paper hats and small toys. Some may also have jokes inside.

CHRISTMAS FACT!

Christmas cards began in England. The first card was sent in England in the 1840s.

CHRISTMAS FACT!

A Yule log is also a dessert made from chocolate cake wrapped in whipped cream. It is decorated to look like a piece of wood.

Christmas Decorations

Evergreens fill homes in England during Christmas. People decorate Christmas trees with lights and ornaments. People also decorate with mistletoe, holly, and ivy. Some families light a Yule log for the holiday. Years ago people believed this big piece of firewood was good luck.

evergreen—a tree or bush that has green needles all year long

Father Christmas

Father Christmas brings holiday joy to kids in England. Father Christmas is much like Santa Claus. He is tall and thin with a long white beard. He wears a long red robe when delivering gifts to children. Father Christmas has also been called Old Father Christmas, Sir Christmas, and Old Winter.

CHRISTMAS FACT!

Early stories of Father Christmas didn't involve gifts. Instead, Father Christmas was said to go door to door, visiting families and sharing food.

Christmas Presents

People around the world give presents on Christmas. This tradition reminds Christians of the gifts the **Three Kings** brought to baby Jesus. In England children write letters to Father Christmas asking for gifts.

Father Christmas brings gifts at night. He fills children's stockings with toys and candy.

Three Kings—three kings who lived 2,000 years ago who are believed to have followed a star to find Jesus in Bethlehem

CHRISTMAS FACT!

In the past, children put letters to Father Christmas in the chimney. They believed smoke carried their wishes to Father Christmas.

CHRISTMAS FACT!

A coin is hidden inside the plum pudding. English people believe that finding the coin brings good luck.

18

Christmas Food

Have you ever tasted plum pudding? How about minced pie or Christmas cake? These sweet treats are holiday favorites in England. Plum pudding is made with spices, nuts, and fruits. Mince pie is a small round pie made from fruit and nuts. It is sometimes made with meat too. Christmas cake is covered with candy and icing. Christmas figures decorate the cake's top.

Christmas Songs

Carols ring out from homes, churches, and streets during Christmastime in England. Carolers go from house to house, singing holiday songs. Sometimes people give carolers hot drinks or money. English people believe caroling brings good luck to homes.

carol—joyful song sung at Christmastime

Hands-On:
MAKE A CHRISTMAS CRACKER

Children in England find tiny toys and surprises when they pop open Christmas crackers. You can share this English tradition with friends. Your crackers won't make a noise, but they will be filled with lots of treats.

What You Need

- 10-inch (25-centimeter) square of wrapping paper
- 1 empty paper tube

- tape or glue
- 2 pieces of ribbon, each about 8 inches (20 cm) long

- candy and small toys
- markers or stickers (optional)

What You Do

1. Wrap the paper around the empty tube tightly. Leave an even amount of paper on each end.
2. Tape or glue the edge of the paper together where it overlaps.
3. Tie one piece of ribbon around the paper at one end of the tube.
4. Fill the tube with candy and small toys.
5. Tie the second piece of ribbon around the paper at the open end of the tube. Decorate the cracker with markers or stickers.
6. To open, pull the paper ends of the tube. When the paper tears, your surprises will pop out!

GLOSSARY

carol (KAYR-uhl)—a joyful song sung at Christmastime

Christian (KRIS-chuhn)—a person who follows a religion based on the teachings of Jesus

evergreen (E-vuhr-green)—a tree or bush that has green needles all year long

Jesus (JEE-zuhs)—the founder of the Christian religion

Three Kings (THREE KINGS)—three kings who lived 2,000 years ago who are believed to have followed a star to find Jesus

tradition (truh-DISH-uhn)—a custom, idea, or belief passed down through time

READ MORE

Banting, Erinn. *England: The Culture*. The Lands, Peoples, and Cultures Series. New York: Crabtree Pub., 2012.

Simmons, Walter. *England*. Exploring Countries. Minneapolis: Bellwether Media, 2011.

Trunkhill, Brenda. *Christmas around the World*. St. Louis: Concordia Publishing House, 2009.

INTERNET SITES

FactHound offers a safe, fun way to find Internet sites related to this book. All of the sites on FactHound have been researched by our staff.

Here's all you do:

Visit *www.facthound.com*

Type in this code: 9781620651414

Check out projects, games and lots more at
www.capstonekids.com

INDEX